# Bond

# *STRETCH*
# Non-verbal Reasoning
## Tests and Papers

## 8–9 years

**Alison Primrose**

Nelson Thornes

Text © Alison Primrose 2013
Original illustrations © Nelson Thornes Ltd 2013

Published in 2013 by:
Nelson Thornes Ltd
Delta Place
27 Bath Road
CHELTENHAM
GL53 7TH
United Kingdom

13 14 15 16 17 / 10 9 8 7 6 5 4 3 2 1

A catalogue record for this book is available from the British Library

ISBN 978 1 4085 1873 1

Page make-up and illustrations by OKS Group

Printed in China by 1010 Printing International Ltd

# *Introduction*

## What is Bond?

The Bond *Stretch* series is a new addition to the Bond range of assessment papers, the number one series for the 11+, selective exams and general practice. Bond *Stretch* is carefully designed to challenge above and beyond the level provided in the regular Bond assessment range.

## How does this book work?

The book contains two distinct sets of papers, along with full answers and a Progress Chart.

- Focus tests, accompanied by advice and directions, are focused on particular (and age-appropriate) non-verbal reasoning question types encountered in the 11+ and other exams, but devised at a higher level than the standard *Assessment Papers*. Each Focus test is designed to help raise a child's skills in the question type, as well as offer plenty of practice for the necessary techniques.

- Mixed papers are full-length tests containing a full range of non-verbal reasoning question types. These are designed to provide rigorous practice for children working at a level higher than that required to pass the 11+ and other non-verbal reasoning tests.

Full answers are provided for both types of test in the middle of the book.

## How much time should the tests take?

The tests are for practice and to reinforce learning, and you may wish to test exam techniques and working to a set time limit. Using the Mixed papers, we would recommend your child spends 25 minutes answering the 36 questions in each paper.

You can reduce the suggested time by five minutes to practise working at speed.

## Using the Progress Chart

The Progress Chart can be used to track Focus test and Mixed paper results over time to monitor how well your child is doing and identify any repeated problems in tackling the different question types.

# Focus test 1   Similarities

Which of the shapes belongs to the group on the left? Circle the letter.

**Example**

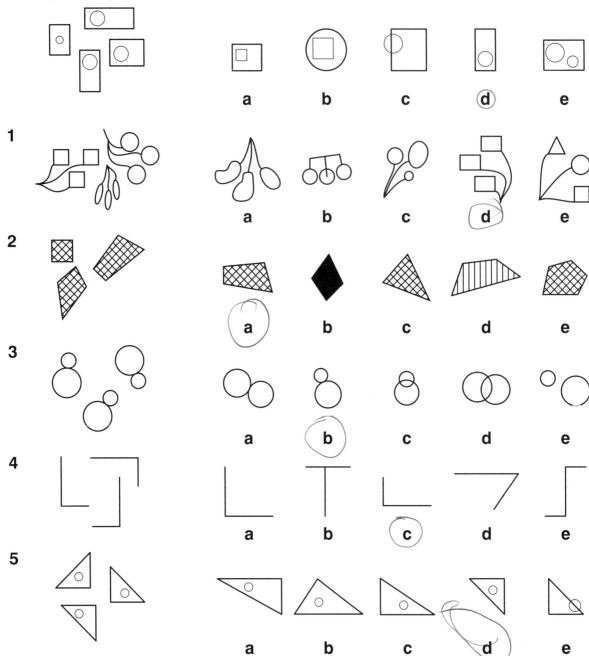

**6**

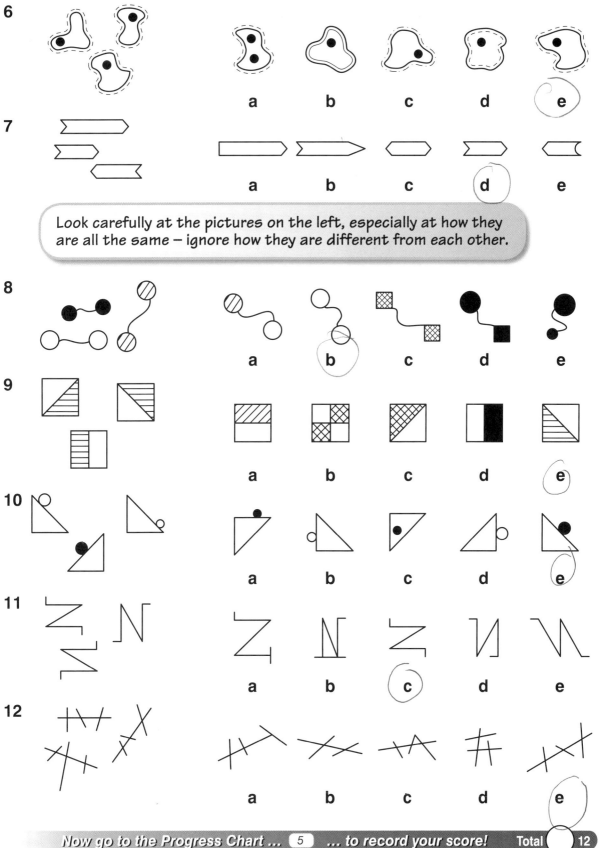

**7**

> Look carefully at the pictures on the left, especially at how they are all the same — ignore how they are different from each other.

**8**

**9**

**10**

**11**

**12**

# Focus test 2   Analogies

Which shape or pattern completes the second pair in the same way as the first pair? Circle the letter.

**Example**

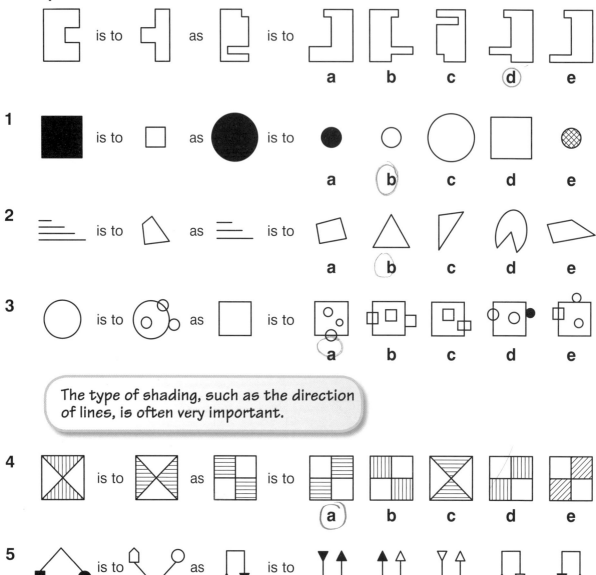

The type of shading, such as the direction of lines, is often very important.

In the next questions, look for any connections between the first two pictures – you need the same connections to complete the second pair.

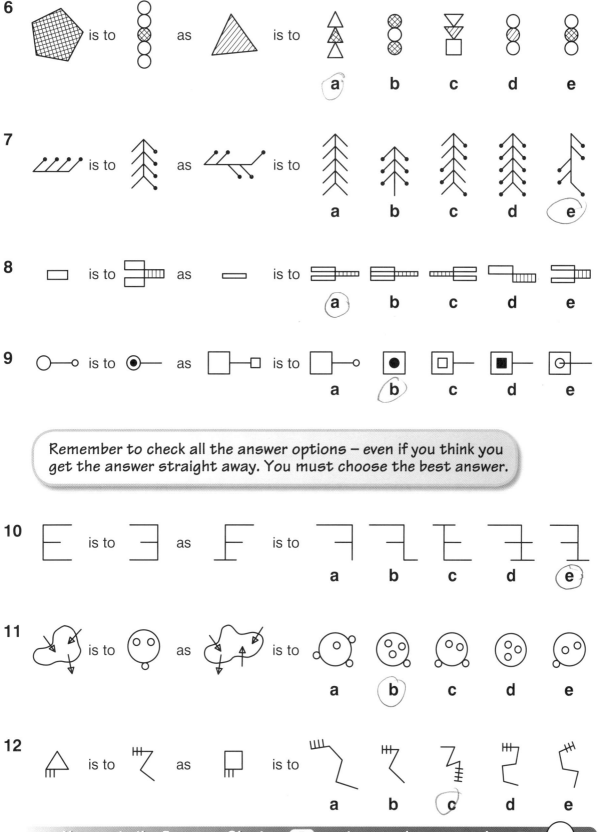

6

7

8

9

Remember to check all the answer options – even if you think you get the answer straight away. You must choose the best answer.

10

11

12

Which code matches the shape or pattern at the end? Circle the letter.

**Example**

With code questions, remember that the first letter will always apply to the same characteristic in the question, such as size or number, and the second letter will apply to a different characteristic.

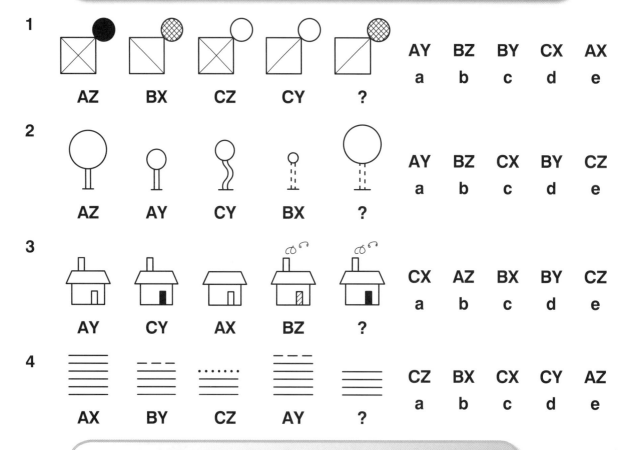

In the next questions, look closely at line lengths and angles, and carefully count elements such as lines, sides or spots.

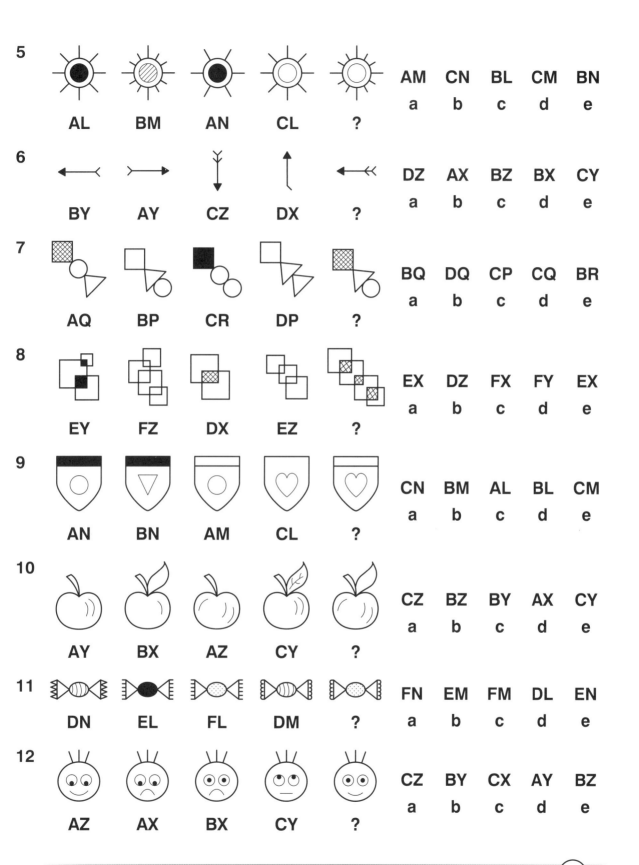

**5**

AL BM AN CL ?

| AM | CN | BL | CM | BN |
|----|----|----|----|----|
| a | b | c | d | e |

**6**

BY AY CZ DX ?

| DZ | AX | BZ | BX | CY |
|----|----|----|----|----|
| a | b | c | d | e |

**7**

AQ BP CR DP ?

| BQ | DQ | CP | CQ | BR |
|----|----|----|----|----|
| a | b | c | d | e |

**8**

EY FZ DX EZ ?

| EX | DZ | FX | FY | EX |
|----|----|----|----|----|
| a | b | c | d | e |

**9**

AN BN AM CL ?

| CN | BM | AL | BL | CM |
|----|----|----|----|----|
| a | b | c | d | e |

**10**

AY BX AZ CY ?

| CZ | BZ | BY | AX | CY |
|----|----|----|----|----|
| a | b | c | d | e |

**11**

DN EL FL DM ?

| FN | EM | FM | DL | EN |
|----|----|----|----|----|
| a | b | c | d | e |

**12**

AZ AX BX CY ?

| CZ | BY | CX | AY | BZ |
|----|----|----|----|----|
| a | b | c | d | e |

# Focus test 4 Cubes

Which net could be folded to make the cube on the left? Circle the letter.

## Example

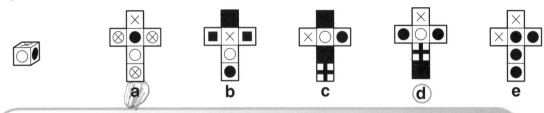

> You have to imagine the net folded up to make a cube (a square box).
> If you find this hard, practise by drawing, cutting out and folding one.

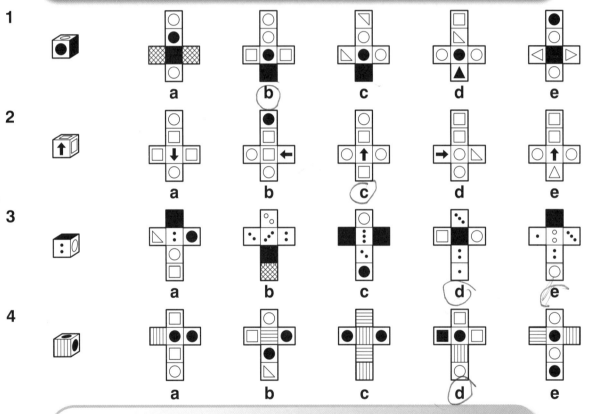

> It helps to learn which squares on the net do not end up being
> next to each other in the cube. This will help you spot them quickly.

**5**

 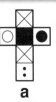 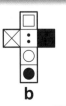 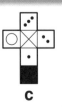 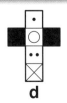 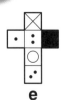

      a           b           c           d           e

**6**

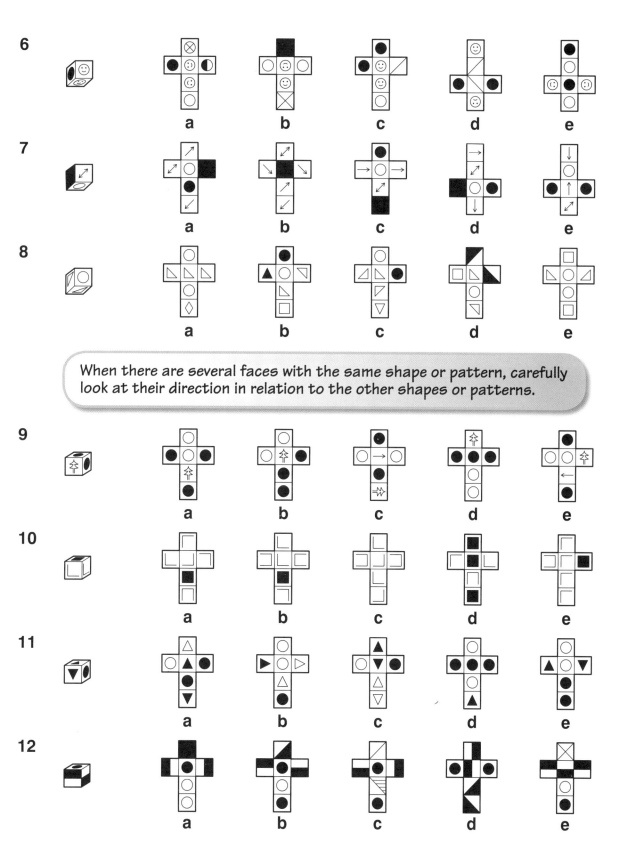

**7**

**8**

When there are several faces with the same shape or pattern, carefully look at their direction in relation to the other shapes or patterns.

**9**

**10**

**11**

**12**

a    b    c    d    e

Which shape on the right is a reflection of the shape on the left?
Circle the letter.

**Example**

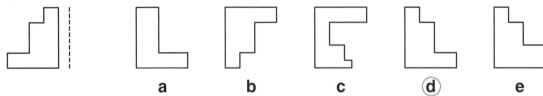

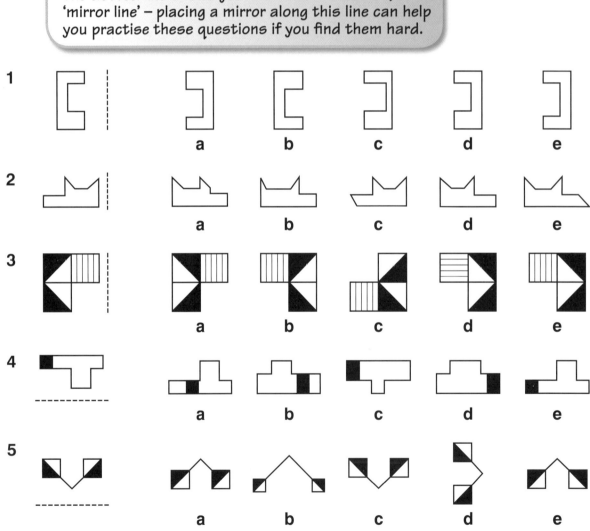

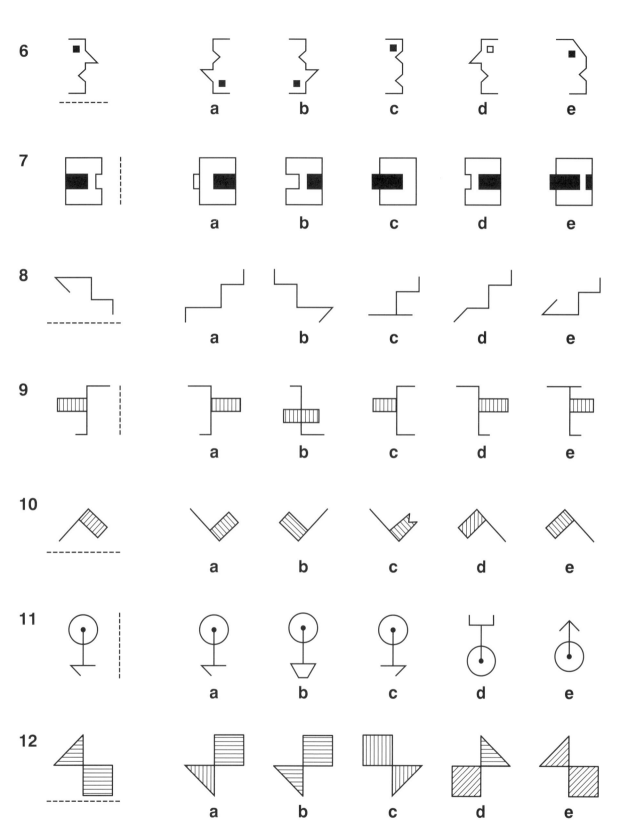

**Sequences**

Which shape or pattern continues or completes the given sequence?
Circle the letter.

**Example**

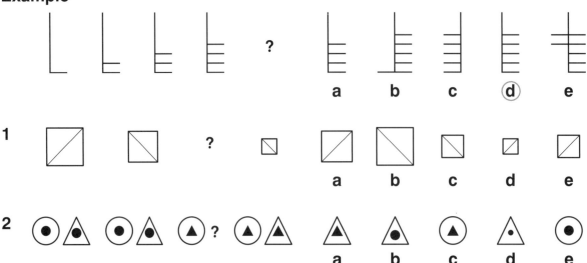

1

2

When making your answer choice, always remember to check the other options – if more than one appears to fit, you must choose the option that fits best.

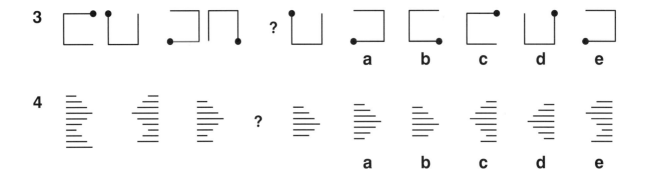

3

4

When completing a sequence, you should look forward to find a pattern and check it by working backwards as well.

5

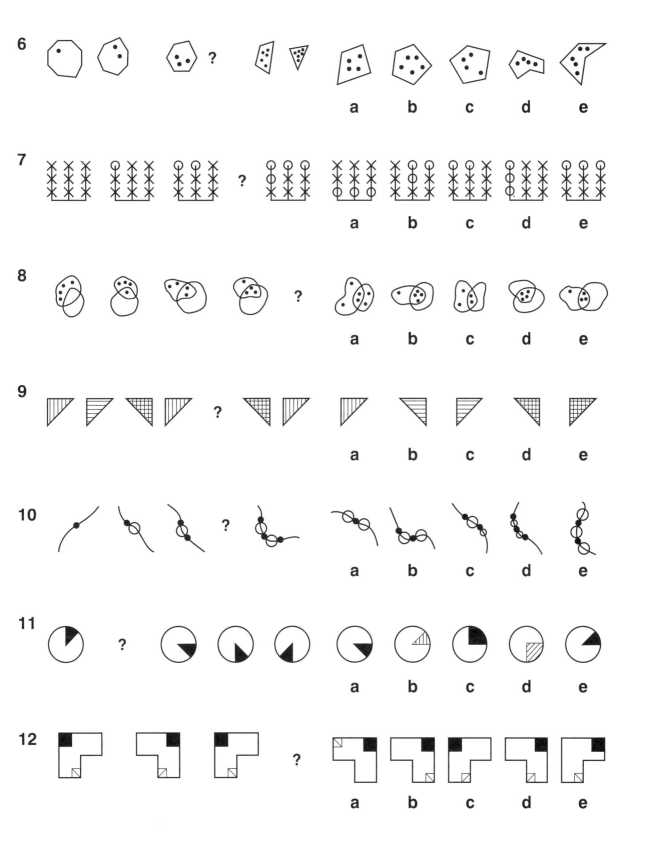

Which pattern completes the grid? Circle the letter.

**Example**

a  b  c  (d)  e

> The whole grid may have a pattern ...

**1**

a  b  c  d  e

**2**

a  b  c  d  e

> ... or the pattern may be in lines.

**3**

a  b  c  d  e

**4**

a  b  c  d  e

**5**

a  b  c  d  e

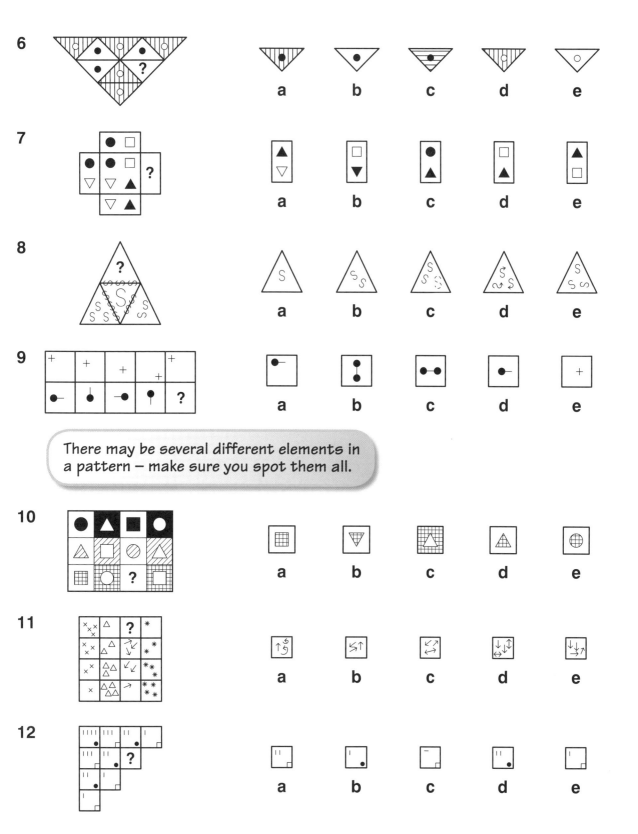

**6**

**7**

**8**

There may be several different elements in a pattern – make sure you spot them all.

**9**

**10**

**11**

**12**

# Focus test 8  Combining shapes

Which pattern is made by putting together the two shapes on the left?
Circle the letter.

**Example**

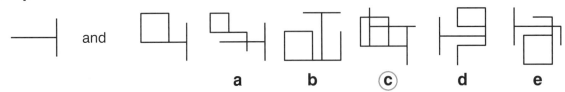

a     b     ⓒ     d     e

> The new pattern must include the two pictures given at the beginning in exactly the same form – there should be no extra lines or shading, etc.

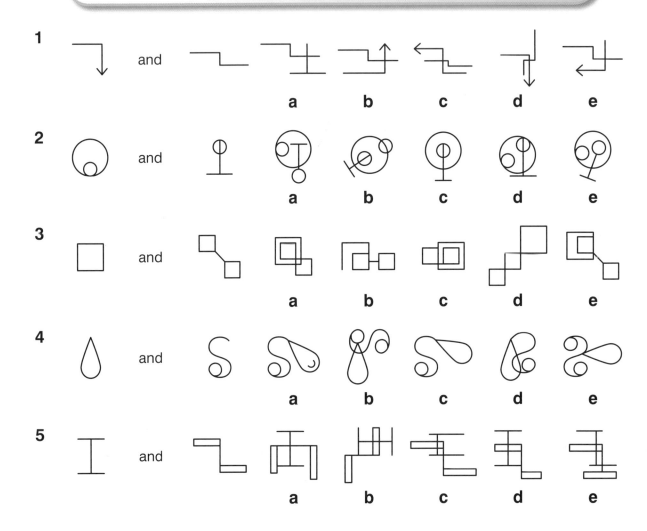

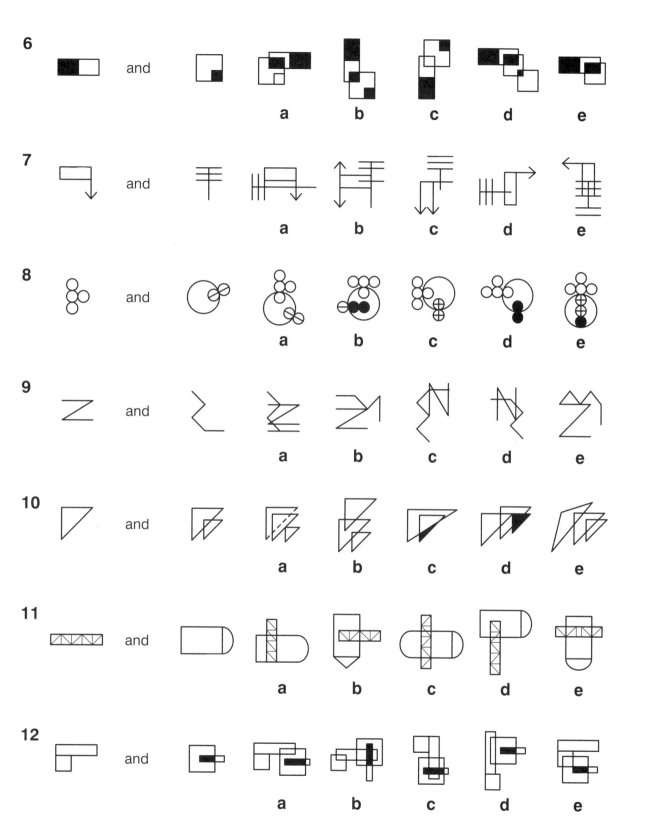

## Mixed paper 1

Which of the shapes belongs to the group on the left? Circle the letter.

**Example**

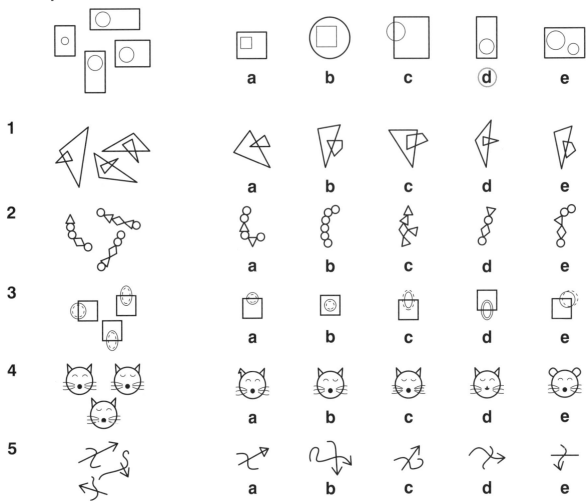

## Mixed paper 1

Which shape or pattern completes the second pair in the same way as the first pair? Circle the letter.

**Example**

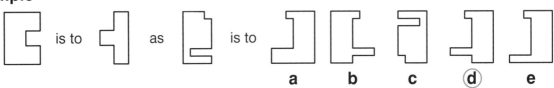

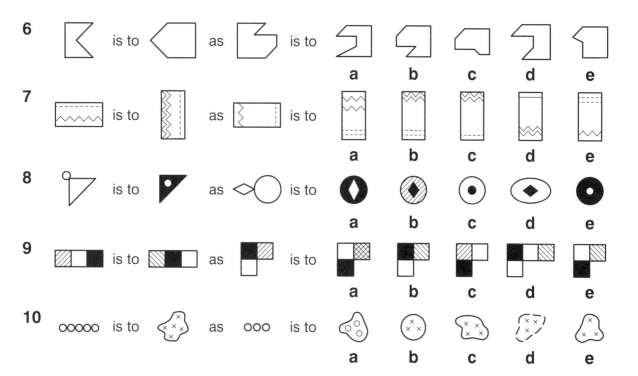

# Mixed paper 1

Which code matches the shape or pattern at the end? Circle the letter.

**Example**

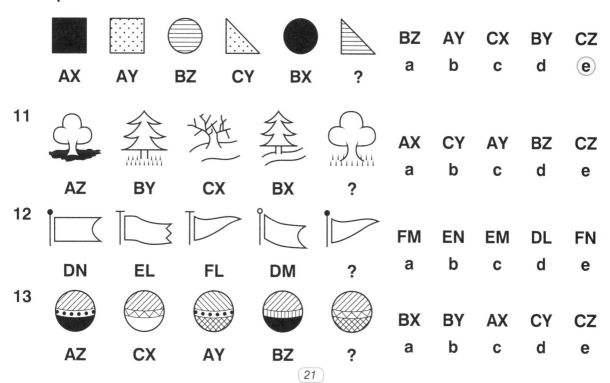

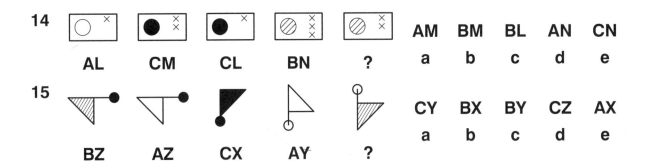

**14**

AL    CM    CL    BN    ?

| AM | BM | BL | AN | CN |
|----|----|----|----|----|
| a | b | c | d | e |

**15**

BZ    AZ    CX    AY    ?

| CY | BX | BY | CZ | AX |
|----|----|----|----|----|
| a | b | c | d | e |

## Mixed paper 1

Which net could be folded to make the cube on the left? Circle the letter.

**Example**

a    b    c    (d)    e

**16**

a    b    c    d    e

**17**

a    b    c    d    e

**18**

a    b    c    d    e

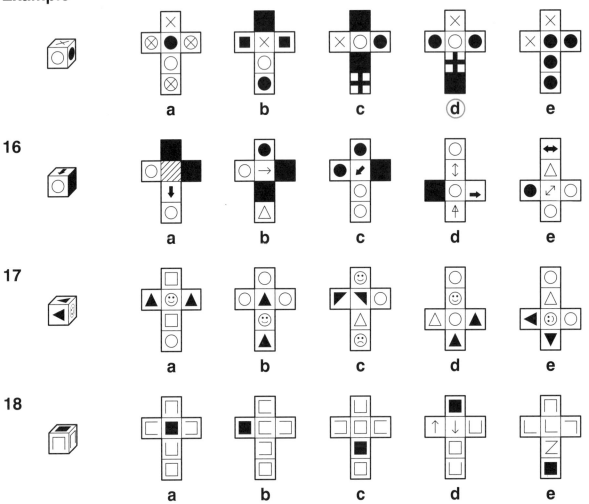

## Focus test 1: Similarities

| | | | |
|---|---|---|---|
| 1 | d | 7 | d |
| 2 | a | 8 | b |
| 3 | b | 9 | e |
| 4 | c | 10 | e |
| 5 | d | 11 | c |
| 6 | e | 12 | e |

## Focus test 2: Analogies

| | | | |
|---|---|---|---|
| 1 | b | 7 | c |
| 2 | c | 8 | a |
| 3 | b | 9 | d |
| 4 | d | 10 | e |
| 5 | c | 11 | b |
| 6 | d | 12 | e |

## Focus test 3: Codes

| | | | |
|---|---|---|---|
| 1 | c | 7 | a |
| 2 | b | 8 | c |
| 3 | e | 9 | e |
| 4 | c | 10 | b |
| 5 | d | 11 | c |
| 6 | c | 12 | e |

## Focus test 4: Cubes

| | | | |
|---|---|---|---|
| 1 | c | 7 | d |
| 2 | b | 8 | b |
| 3 | d | 9 | e |
| 4 | b | 10 | e |
| 5 | e | 11 | c |
| 6 | c | 12 | d |

## Focus test 5: Reflections

| | | | |
|---|---|---|---|
| 1 | d | 7 | d |
| 2 | d | 8 | e |
| 3 | e | 9 | d |
| 4 | e | 10 | a |
| 5 | e | 11 | c |
| 6 | b | 12 | b |

## Focus test 6: Sequences

| | | | |
|---|---|---|---|
| 1 | e | 7 | e |
| 2 | a | 8 | d |
| 3 | c | 9 | c |
| 4 | d | 10 | b |
| 5 | e | 11 | e |
| 6 | c | 12 | d |

## Focus test 7: Grids

| | | | |
|---|---|---|---|
| 1 | c | 7 | d |
| 2 | c | 8 | e |
| 3 | d | 9 | d |
| 4 | a | 10 | d |
| 5 | c | 11 | e |
| 6 | b | 12 | e |

## Focus test 8: Combining shapes

| | | | |
|---|---|---|---|
| 1 | e | 7 | d |
| 2 | d | 8 | a |
| 3 | e | 9 | d |
| 4 | c | 10 | b |
| 5 | b | 11 | d |
| 6 | c | 12 | e |

Bond STRETCH Non-verbal Reasoning Tests and Papers 8–9 years

## Mixed paper 1

1 d
2 e
3 a
4 b
5 c
6 d
7 c
8 a
9 e
10 e
11 c
12 e
13 d
14 b
15 c
16 a
17 e
18 b
19 c
20 d
21 c
22 d
23 d
24 b
25 d
26 c
27 e
28 d
29 c
30 d
31 a
32 a
33 b
34 d
35 a
36 e

## Mixed paper 2

1 d
2 a
3 e
4 c
5 c
6 e
7 b
8 a
9 d
10 d
11 b
12 d
13 e
14 c
15 e
16 e
17 b
18 c
19 b
20 c
21 c
22 d
23 e

| | |
|---|---|
| **24** d | **17** d |
| **25** c | **18** e |
| **26** c | **19** c |
| **27** a | **20** e |
| **28** e | **21** d |
| **29** c | **22** b |
| **30** a | **23** d |
| **31** c | **24** b |
| **32** d | **25** c |
| **33** e | **26** d |
| **34** c | **27** e |
| **35** e | **28** b |
| **36** c | **29** c |
| | **30** e |

## Mixed paper 3

| | |
|---|---|
| **1** e | **31** d |
| **2** c | **32** c |
| **3** a | **33** c |
| **4** d | **34** e |
| **5** c | **35** b |
| **6** b | **36** c |
| **7** e | |

## Mixed paper 4

| | |
|---|---|
| **8** b | **1** d |
| **9** c | **2** e |
| **10** d | **3** c |
| **11** d | **4** b |
| **12** c | **5** d |
| **13** a | **6** c |
| **14** c | **7** d |
| **15** b | **8** d |
| **16** a | **9** b |

| | | | |
|---|---|---|---|
| **10** | c | **24** | c |
| **11** | c | **25** | a |
| **12** | e | **26** | e |
| **13** | b | **27** | c |
| **14** | a | **28** | b |
| **15** | e | **29** | b |
| **16** | b | **30** | e |
| **17** | c | **31** | c |
| **18** | e | **32** | c |
| **19** | d | **33** | e |
| **20** | b | **34** | b |
| **21** | d | **35** | d |
| **22** | c | **36** | d |
| **23** | e | | |

**19**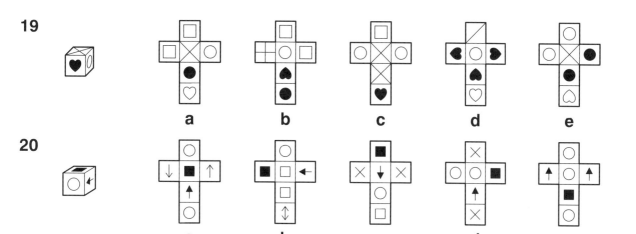

a      b      c      d      e

**20**

a      b      c      d      e

# Mixed paper 1

Which shape on the right is a reflection of the shape on the left? Circle the letter.

**Example**

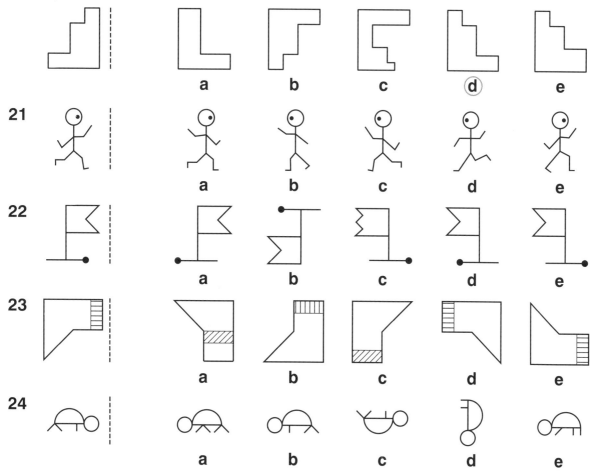

a      b      c      (d)      e

**21**

a      b      c      d      e

**22**

a      b      c      d      e

**23**

a      b      c      d      e

**24**

a      b      c      d      e

# Mixed paper 1

Which shape or pattern continues or completes the given sequence?
Circle the letter.

**Example**

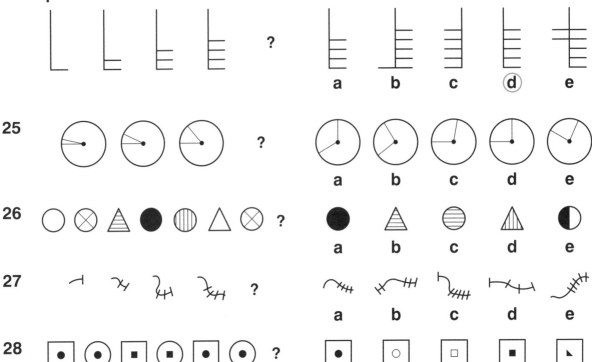

25

26

27

28

# Mixed paper 1

Which pattern completes the grid? Circle the letter.

**Example**

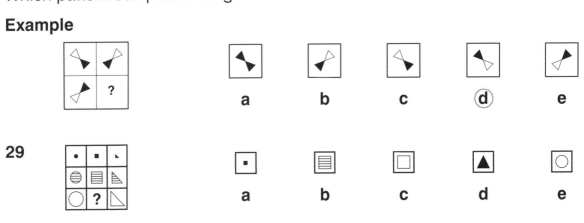

29

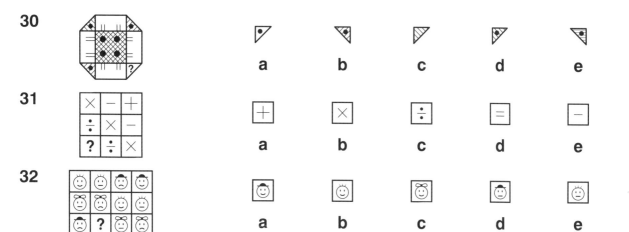

**30**    a      b      c      d      e

**31**    a      b      c      d      e

**32**    a      b      c      d      e

# Mixed paper 1

Which pattern is made by putting together the two shapes on the left?
Circle the letter.

**Example**

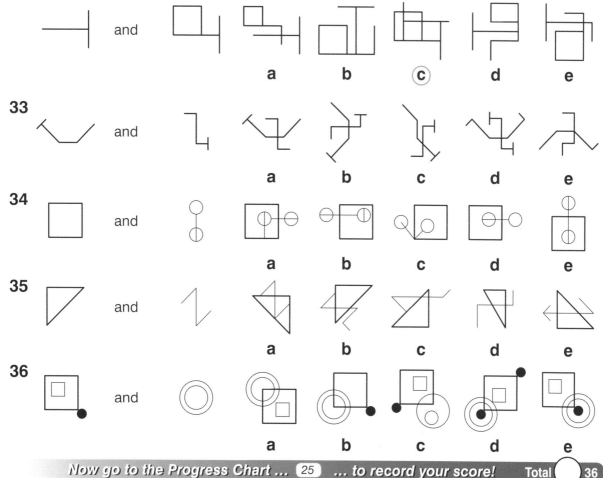

# Mixed paper 2

Which of the shapes belongs to the group on the left? Circle the letter.

**Example**

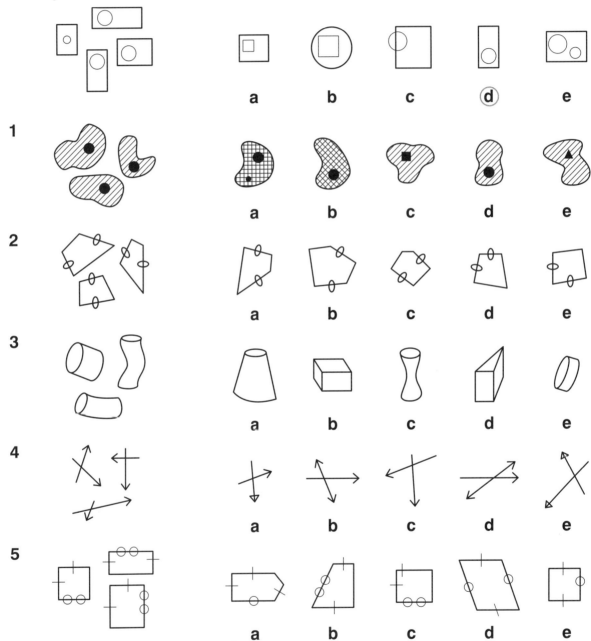

## Mixed paper 2

Which shape or pattern completes the second pair in the same way as the first pair? Circle the letter.

### Example

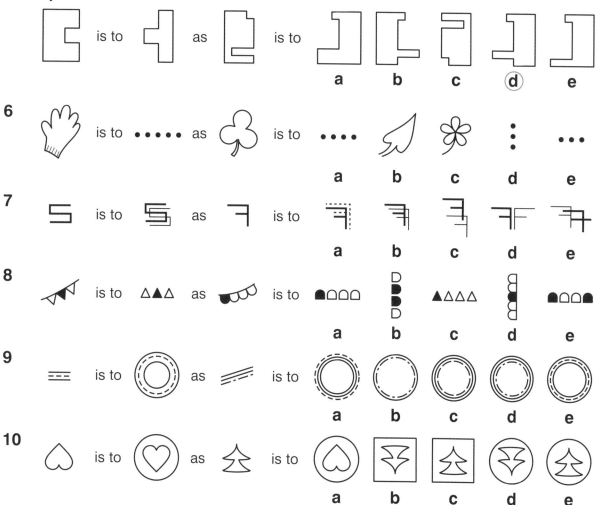

## Mixed paper 2

Which code matches the shape or pattern at the end? Circle the letter.

### Example

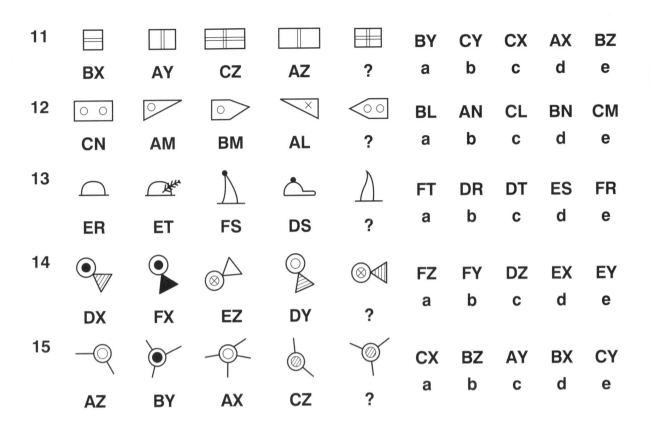

11    BX    AY    CZ    AZ    ?

| BY | CY | CX | AX | BZ |
|----|----|----|----|----|
| a | b | c | d | e |

12    CN    AM    BM    AL    ?

| BL | AN | CL | BN | CM |
|----|----|----|----|----|
| a | b | c | d | e |

13    ER    ET    FS    DS    ?

| FT | DR | DT | ES | FR |
|----|----|----|----|----|
| a | b | c | d | e |

14    DX    FX    EZ    DY    ?

| FZ | FY | DZ | EX | EY |
|----|----|----|----|----|
| a | b | c | d | e |

15    AZ    BY    AX    CZ    ?

| CX | BZ | AY | BX | CY |
|----|----|----|----|----|
| a | b | c | d | e |

## Mixed paper 2

Which net could be folded to make the cube on the left? Circle the letter.

**Example**

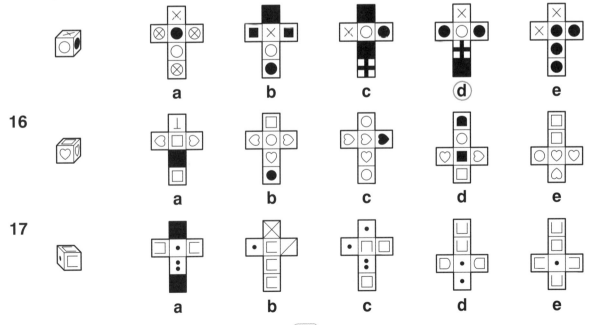

16    a    b    c    d    e

17    a    b    c    d    e

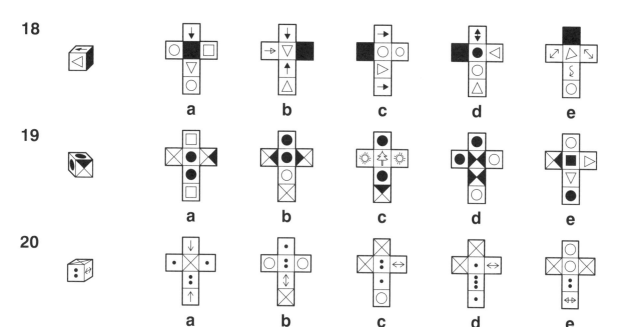

## Mixed paper 2

Which shape on the right is a reflection of the shape on the left? Circle the letter.

**Example**

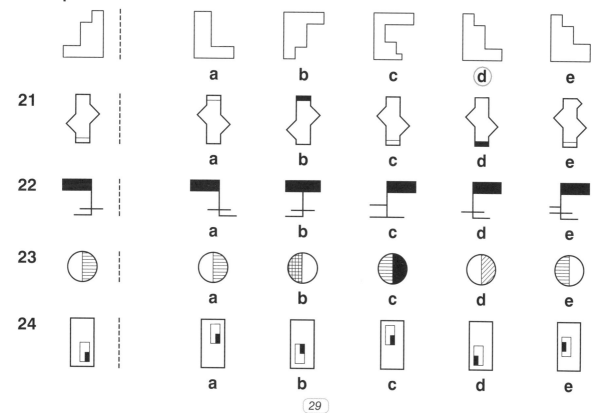

# Mixed paper 2

Which shape or pattern continues or completes the given sequence?
Circle the letter.

**Example**

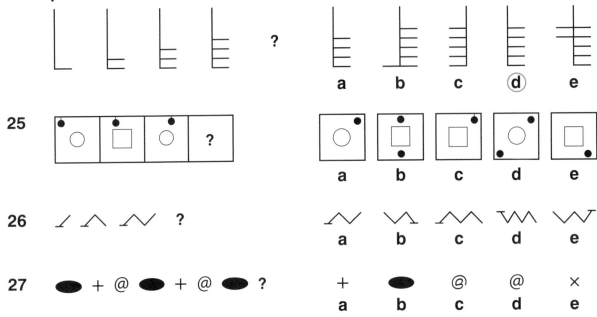

**25**

**26**

**27**

**28**

# Mixed paper 2

Which pattern completes the grid? Circle the letter.

**Example**

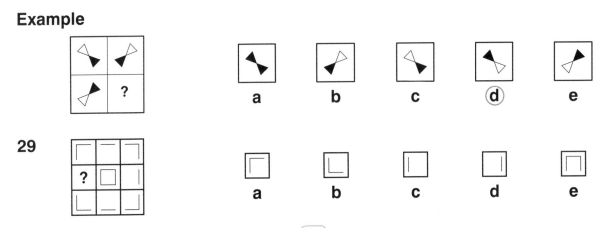

**29**

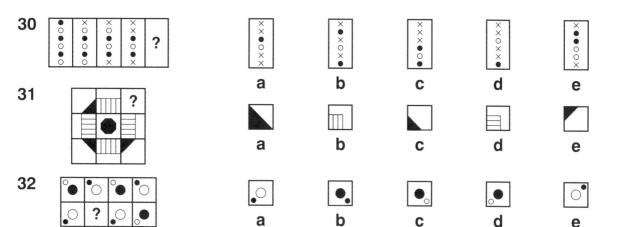

**30**   a   b   c   d   e

**31**   a   b   c   d   e

**32**   a   b   c   d   e

## Mixed paper 2

Which pattern is made by putting together the two shapes on the left?
Circle the letter.

**Example**

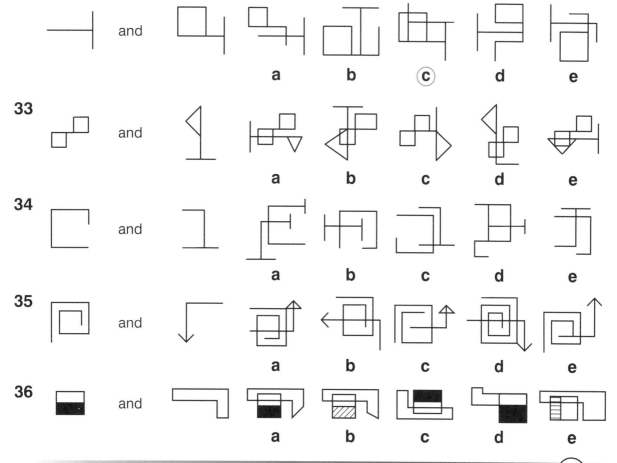

and   a   b   **c**   d   e

**33**   and   a   b   c   d   e

**34**   and   a   b   c   d   e

**35**   and   a   b   c   d   e

**36**   and   a   b   c   d   e

# Mixed paper 3

Which of the shapes belongs to the group on the left? Circle the letter.

**Example**

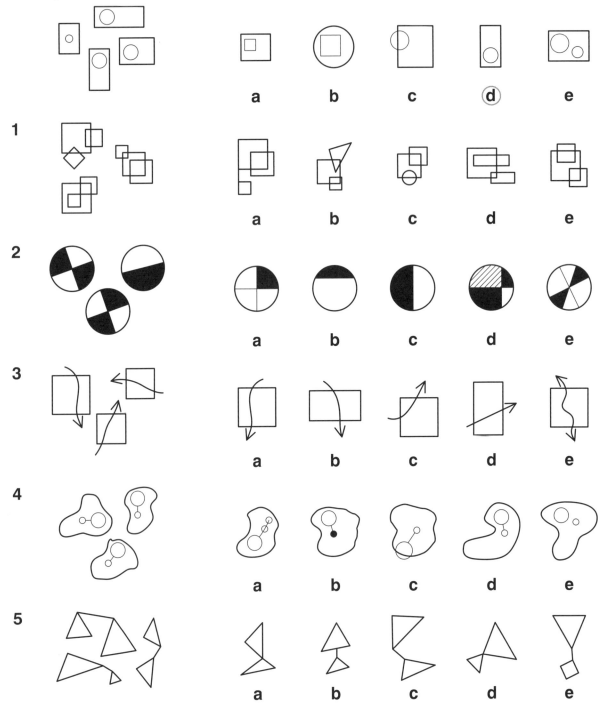

Which shape or pattern completes the second pair in the same way as the first pair? Circle the letter.

**Example**

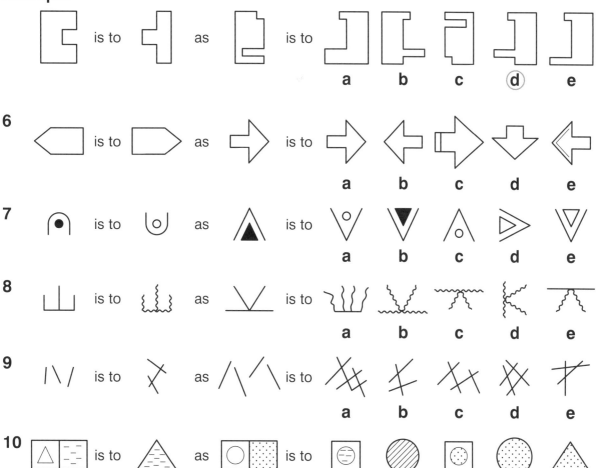

**6**

**7**

**8**

**9**

**10**

Which code matches the shape or pattern at the end? Circle the letter.

**Example**

| AX | AY | BZ | CY | BX | ? |
| --- | --- | --- | --- | --- | --- |

| BZ | AY | CX | BY | CZ |
| --- | --- | --- | --- | --- |
| a | b | c | d | (e) |

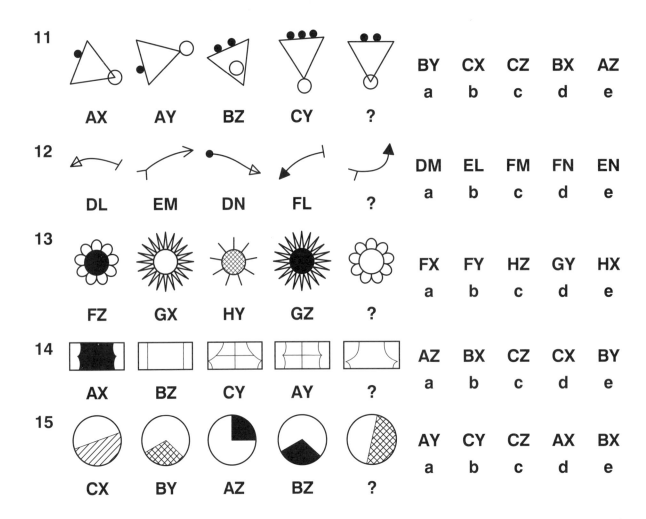

**11**

BY CX CZ BX AZ
a   b   c   d   e

AX   AY   BZ   CY   ?

**12**

DM EL FM FN EN
a   b   c   d   e

DL   EM   DN   FL   ?

**13**

FX FY HZ GY HX
a   b   c   d   e

FZ   GX   HY   GZ   ?

**14**

AZ BX CZ CX BY
a   b   c   d   e

AX   BZ   CY   AY   ?

**15**

AY CY CZ AX BX
a   b   c   d   e

CX   BY   AZ   BZ   ?

## Mixed paper 3

Which net could be folded to make the cube on the left? Circle the letter.

**Example**

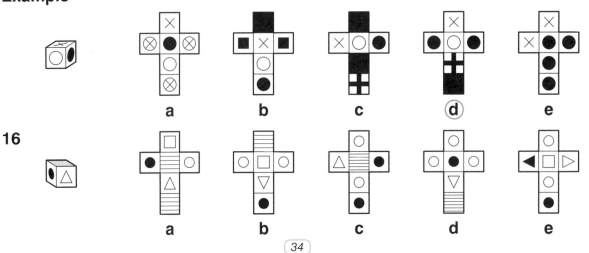

a   b   c   (d)   e

**16**

a   b   c   d   e

**17**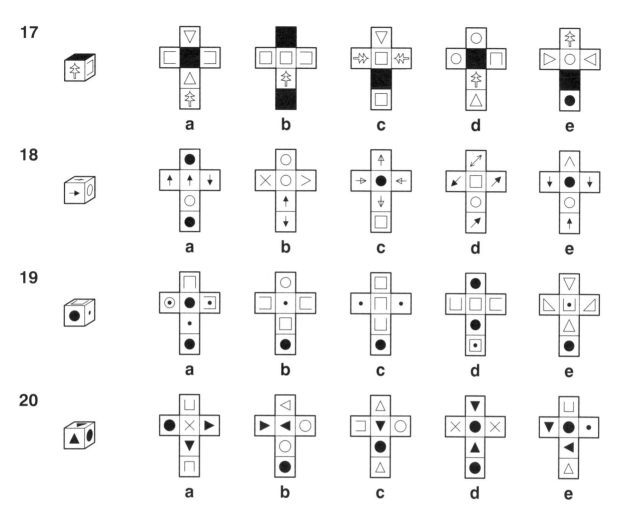

a    b    c    d    e

**18**

a    b    c    d    e

**19**

a    b    c    d    e

**20**

a    b    c    d    e

# Mixed paper 3

Which shape on the right is a reflection of the shape on the left?
Circle the letter.

**Example**

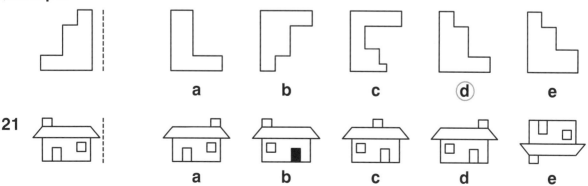

a    b    c    (d)    e

**21**

a    b    c    d    e

**22**

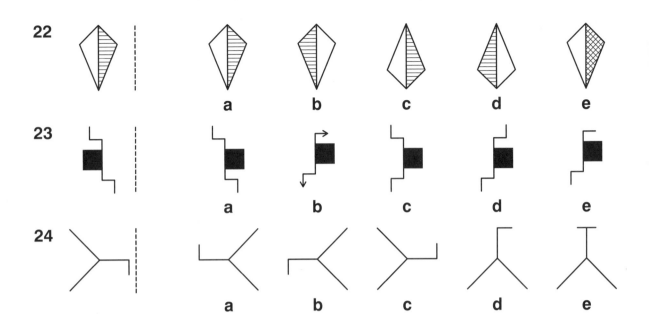

a     b     c     d     e

**23**

a     b     c     d     e

**24**

a     b     c     d     e

# Mixed paper 3

Which shape or pattern continues or completes the given sequence?
Circle the letter.

**Example**

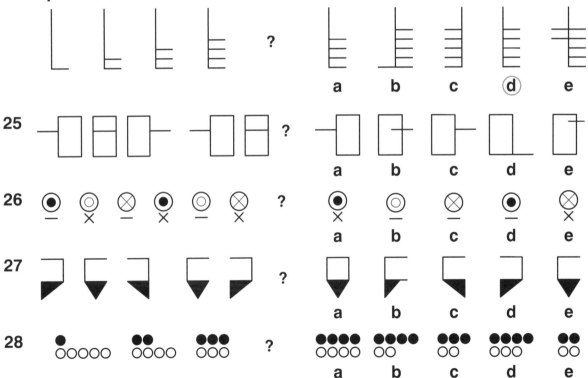

a     b     c     (d)     e

**25** ?

a     b     c     d     e

**26** ?

a     b     c     d     e

**27** ?

a     b     c     d     e

**28** ?

a     b     c     d     e

# Mixed paper 3

Which pattern completes the grid? Circle the letter.

**Example**

a     b     c     (d)     e

**29**

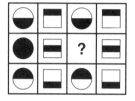

a     b     c     d     e

**30**

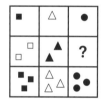

a     b     c     d     e

**31**

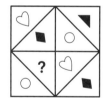

a     b     c     d     e

**32**

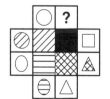

a     b     c     d     e

# Mixed paper 3

Which pattern is made by putting together the two shapes on the left?
Circle the letter.

**Example**

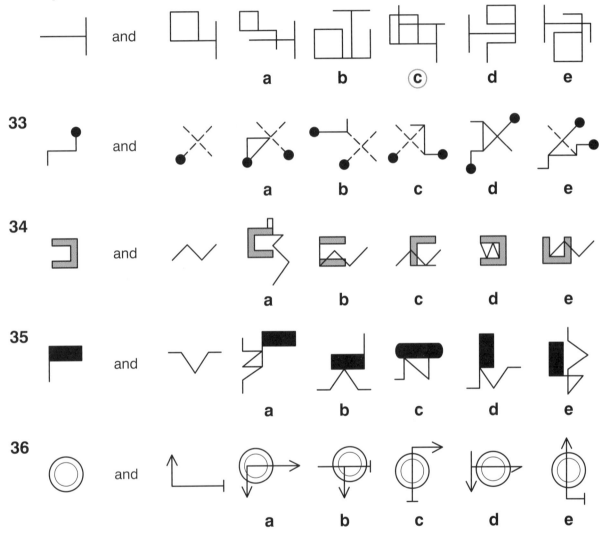

# Mixed paper 4

Which of the shapes belongs to the group on the left? Circle the letter.

**Example**

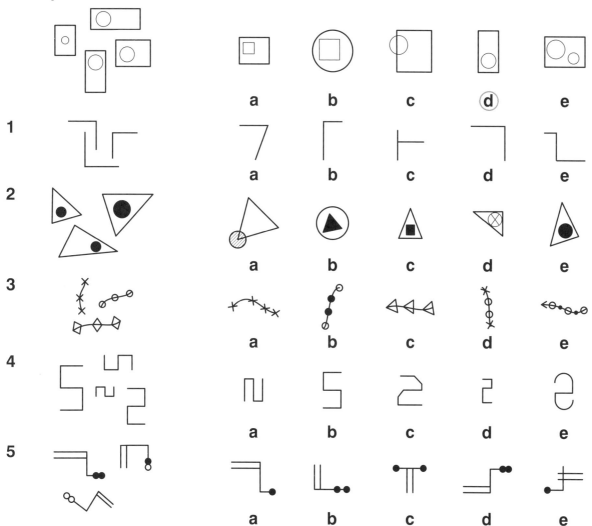

# Mixed paper 4

Which shape or pattern completes the second pair in the same way as the first pair? Circle the letter.

**Example**

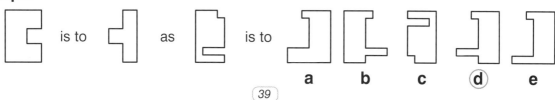

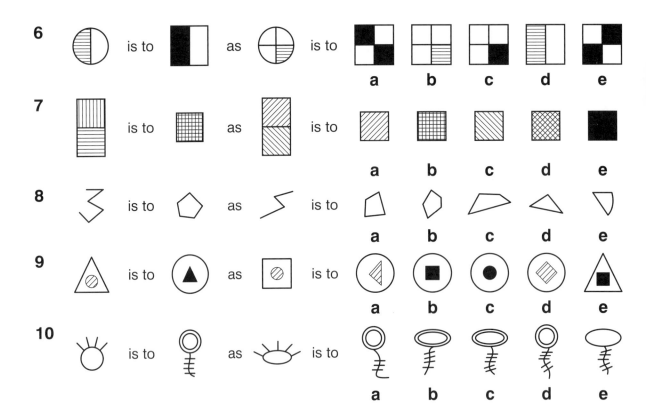

## Mixed paper 4

Which code matches the shape or pattern at the end? Circle the letter.

**Example**

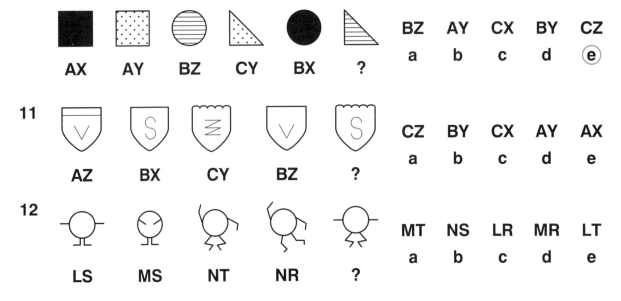

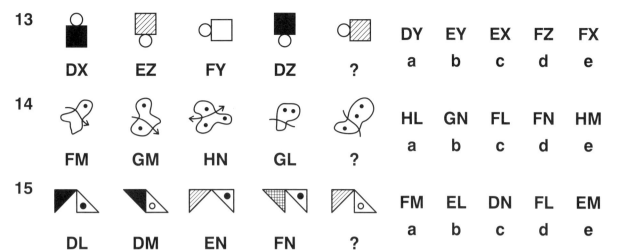

**13**

DX    EZ    FY    DZ    ?

| DY | EY | EX | FZ | FX |
|----|----|----|----|----|
| a | b | c | d | e |

**14**

FM    GM    HN    GL    ?

| HL | GN | FL | FN | HM |
|----|----|----|----|----|
| a | b | c | d | e |

**15**

DL    DM    EN    FN    ?

| FM | EL | DN | FL | EM |
|----|----|----|----|----|
| a | b | c | d | e |

# Mixed paper 4

Which net could be folded to make the cube on the left? Circle the letter.

## Example

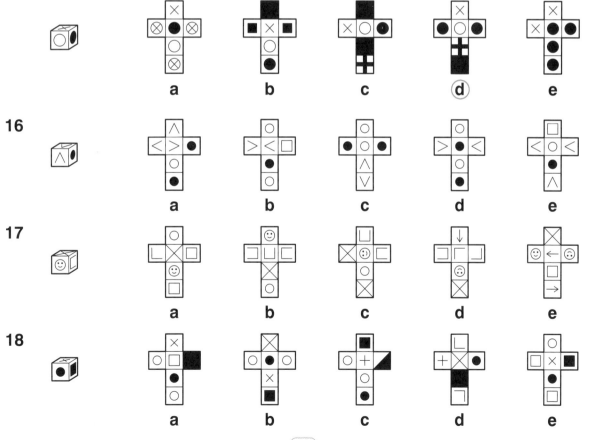

**16**

a    b    c    d    e

**17**

a    b    c    d    e

**18**

a    b    c    d    e

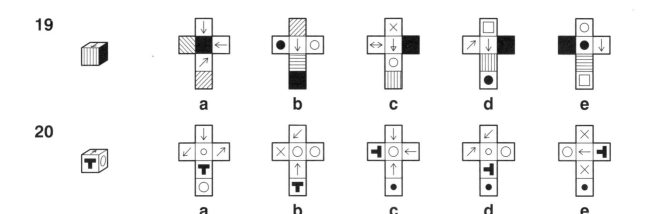

## Mixed paper 4

Which shape on the right is a reflection of the shape on the left? Circle the letter.

**Example**

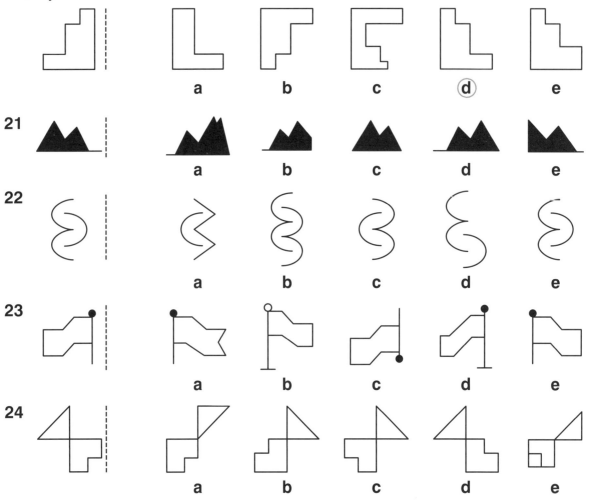

# Mixed paper 4

Which shape or pattern continues or completes the given sequence?
Circle the letter.

**Example**

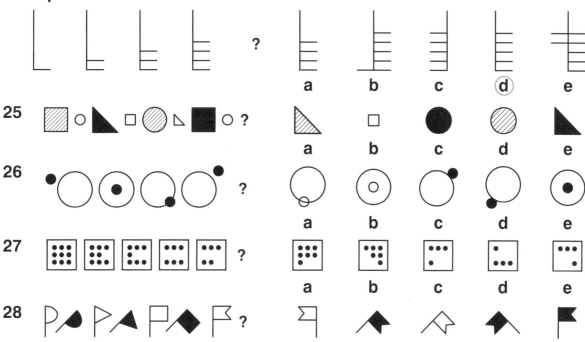

# Mixed paper 4

Which pattern completes the grid? Circle the letter.

**Example**

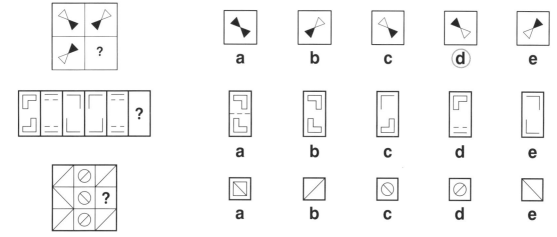

**31**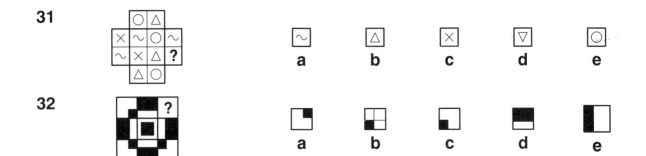

**32**

## Mixed paper 4

Which pattern is made by putting together the two shapes on the left?
Circle the letter.

**Example**

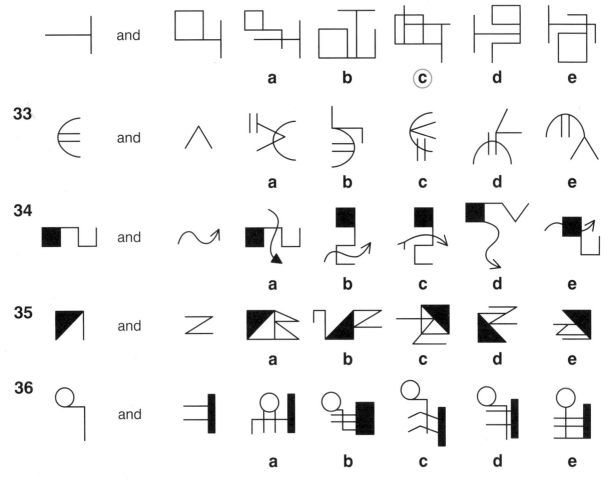

**33**

**34**

**35**

**36**